BIG-NOTE PIANO

QUEEN

Cover photo: Getty Images/ullstein bild/contributor

ISBN 978-1-4950-8965-7

7777 W. BLUEMOUND RD. P.O. BOX 13819 MILWAUKEE, WI 53213

In Australia Contact:
Hal Leonard Australia Pty. Ltd.
4 Lentara Court
Cheltenham, Victoria, 3192 Australia
Email: ausadmin@halleonard.com.au

Visit Hal Leonard Online at
www.halleonard.com

ANOTHER ONE BITES THE DUST

Words and Music by
JOHN DEACON

D.S. al Coda

oth - er one bites the dust.

BOHEMIAN RHAPSODY

Words and Music by
FREDDIE MERCURY

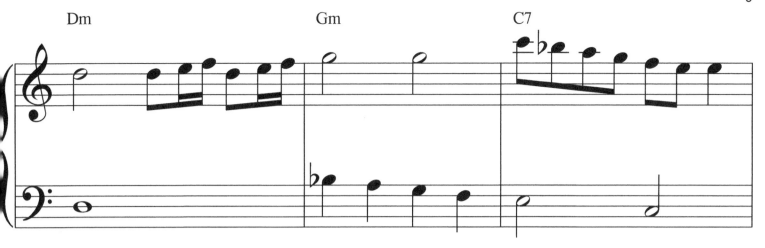

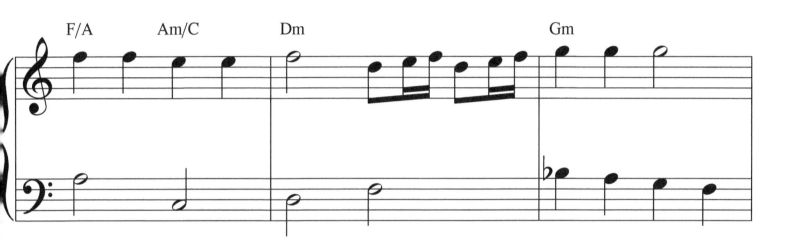

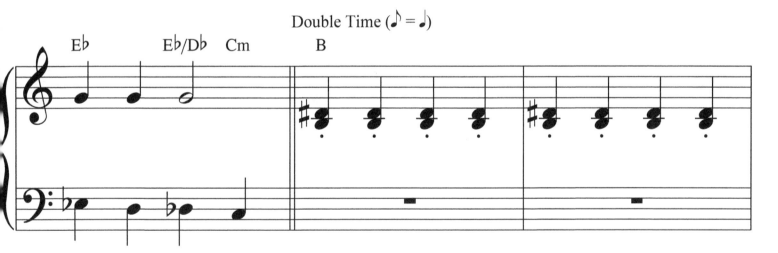

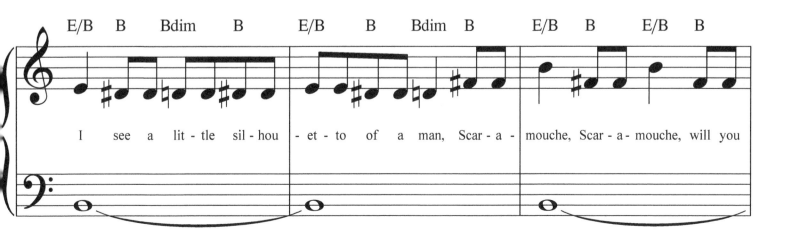

I see a lit-tle sil-hou - et-to of a man, Scar-a-mouche, Scar-a-mouche, will you

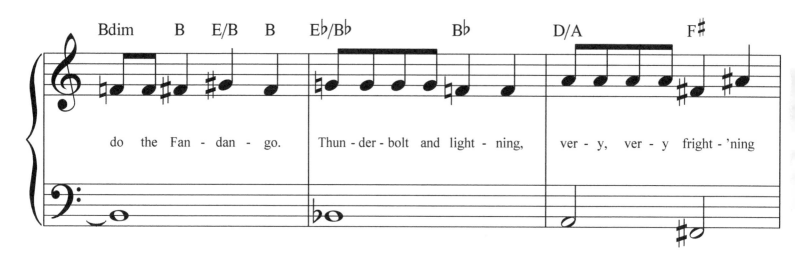

do the Fan - dan - go. Thun - der - bolt and light - ning, ver - y, ver - y fright - 'ning

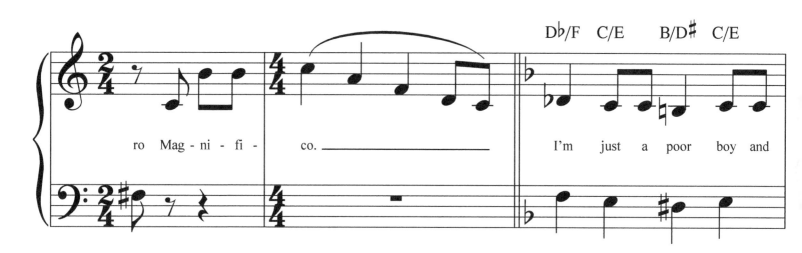

me. (Gal - li - le - o.) Gal - li - le - o. (Gal - li - le - o.) Gal - li - le - o, Gal - li - le - o Fig - a -

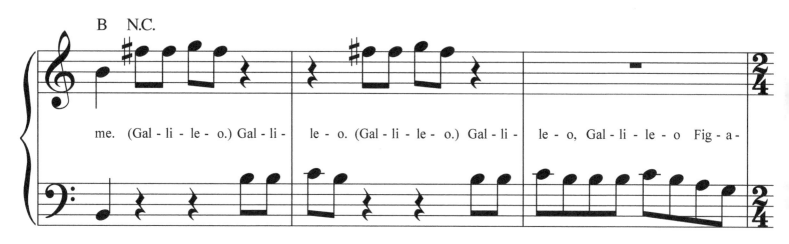

ro Mag - ni - fi - co. _____ I'm just a poor boy and

no - bod - y loves me. He's just a poor boy from a poor fam - i - ly.

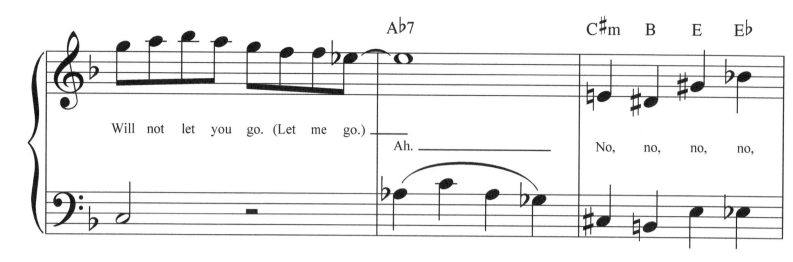

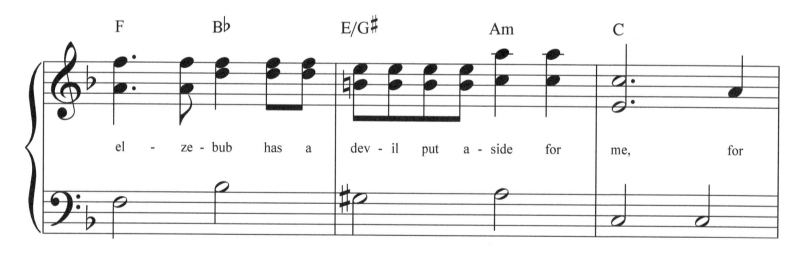

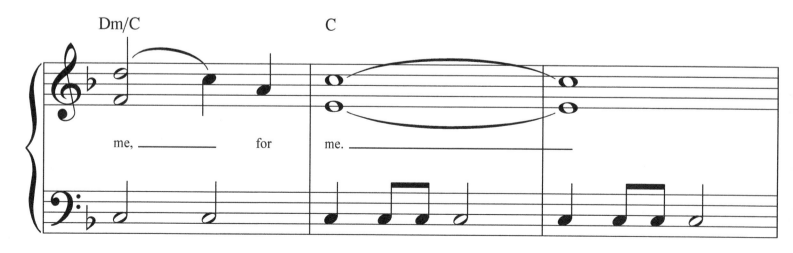

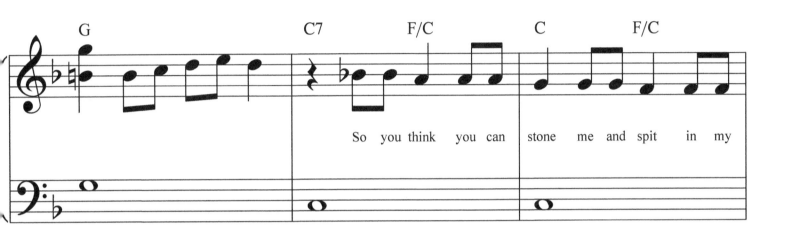

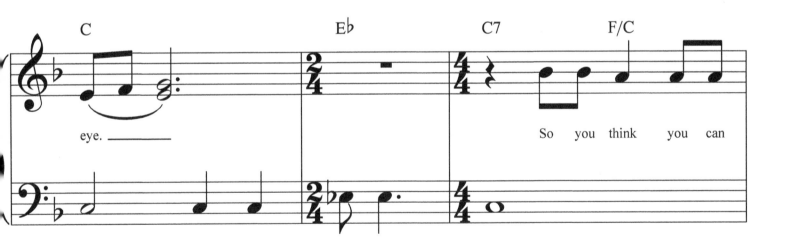

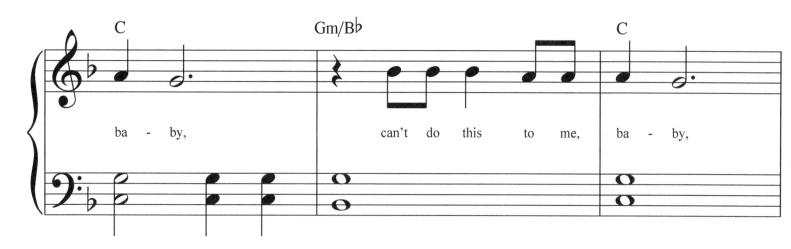

ba - by, can't do this to me, ba - by,

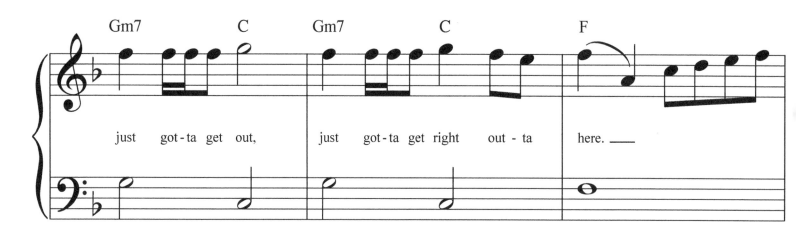

just got-ta get out, just got-ta get right out - ta here. ___

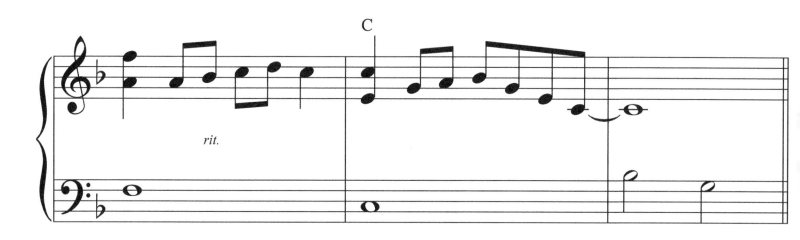

rit.

Slowly, a tempo

CRAZY LITTLE THING CALLED LOVE

Words and Music by
FREDDIE MERCURY

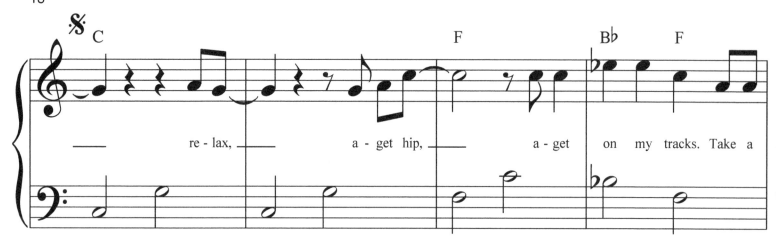

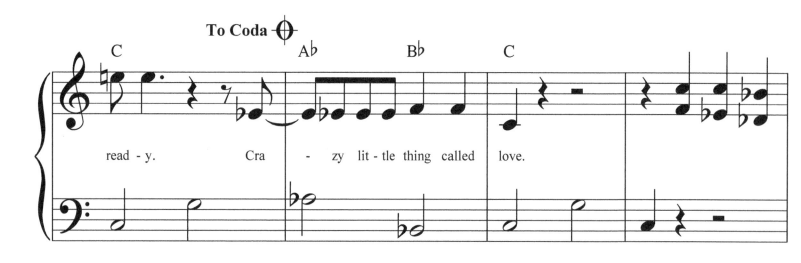

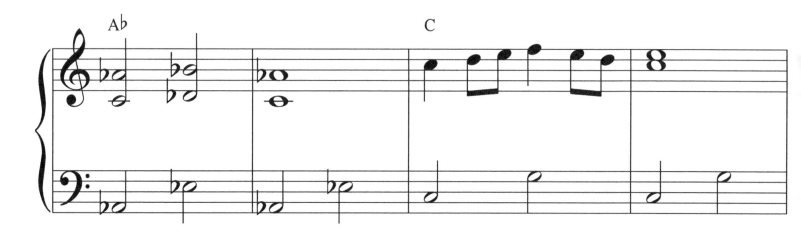

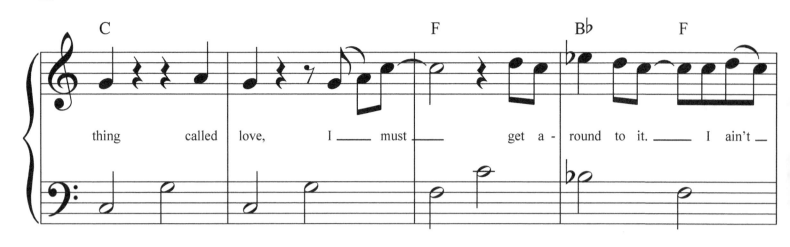

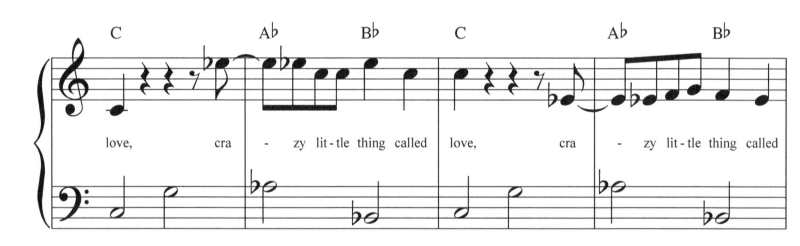

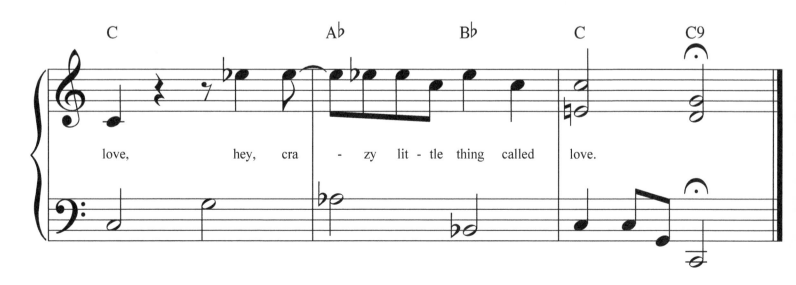

DON'T STOP ME NOW

Words and Music by
FREDDIE MERCURY

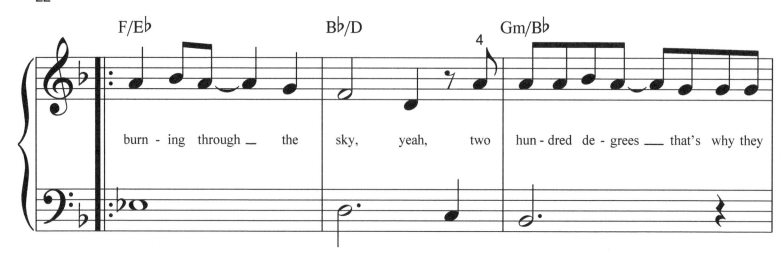

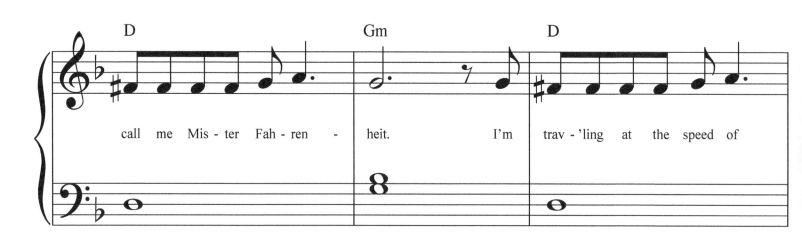

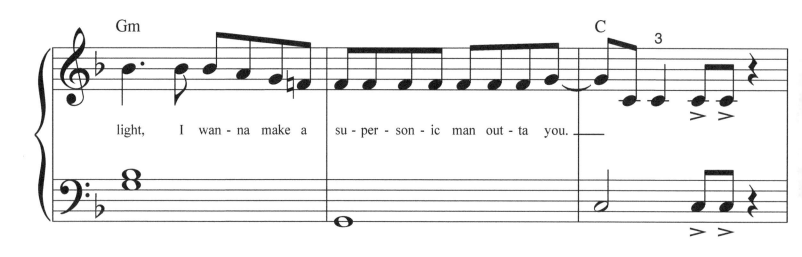

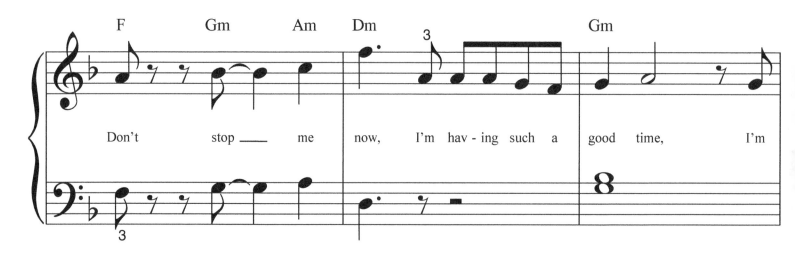

KILLER QUEEN

Words and Music by
FREDDIE MERCURY

SOMEBODY TO LOVE

Words and Music by
FREDDIE MERCURY

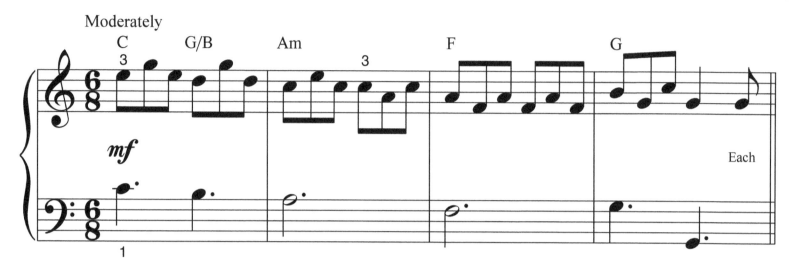

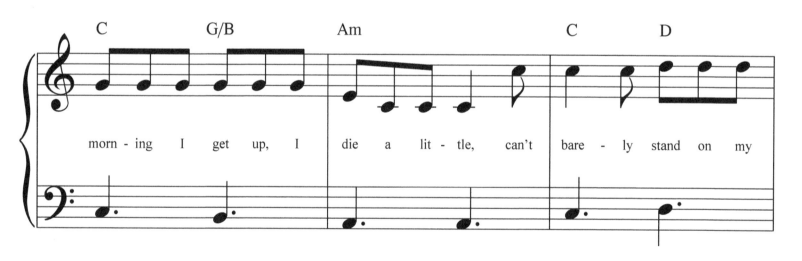

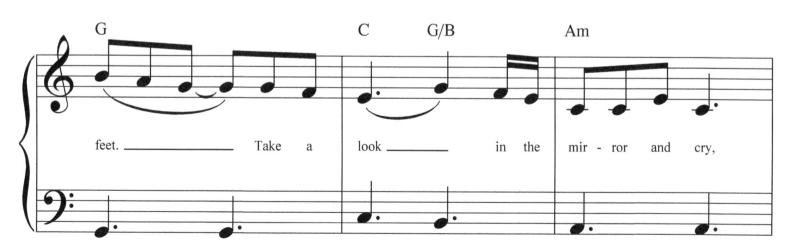

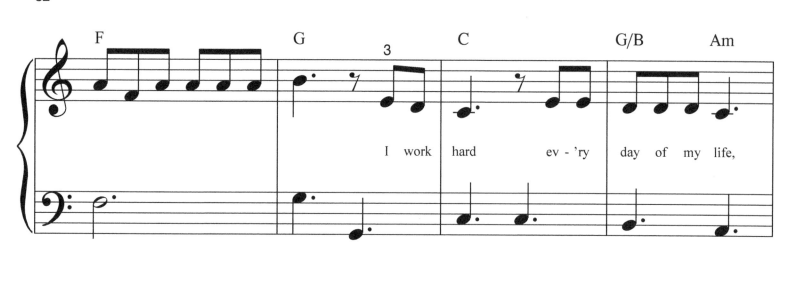

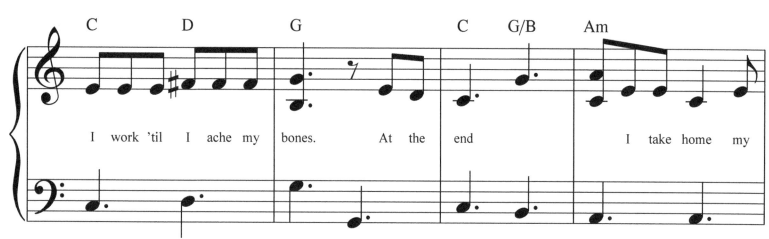

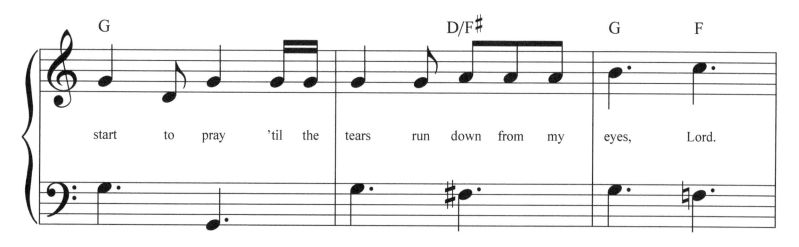

Some - bod - y, _____ some - bod - y, _____ can an - y - bod - y

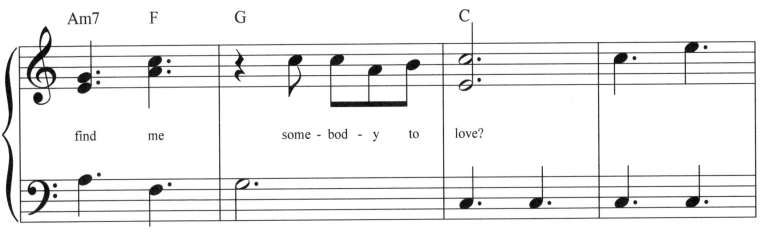

find me some - bod - y to love?

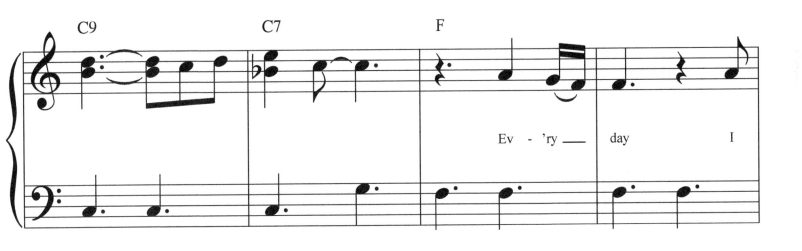

Ev - 'ry _____ day I

try and I try and I try, _____ but ev - 'ry - bod - y

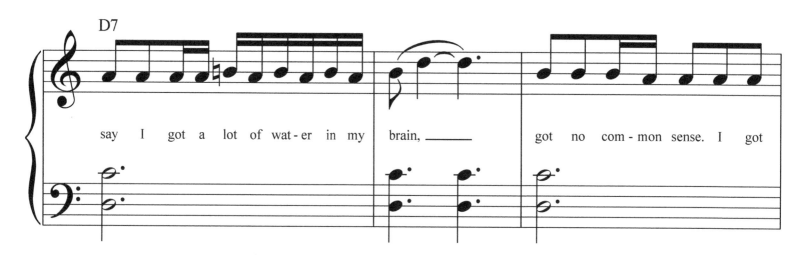

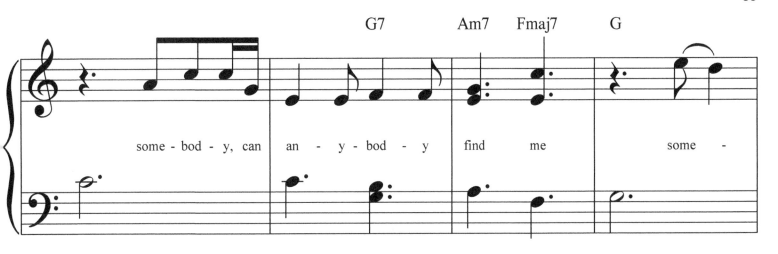

some - bod - y, can an - y - bod - y find me some -

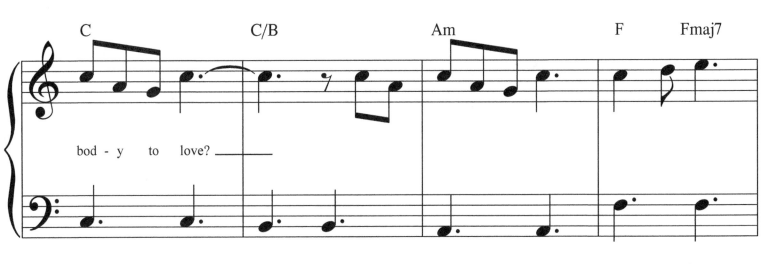

bod - y to love? _____

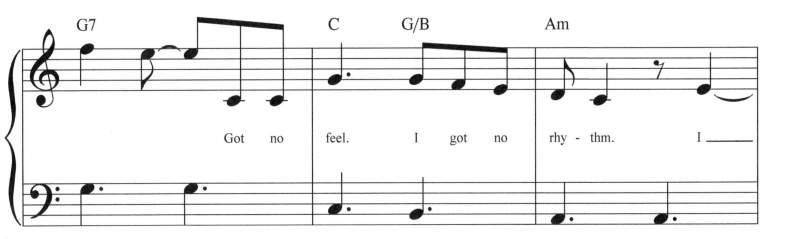

Got no feel. I got no rhy - thm. I _____

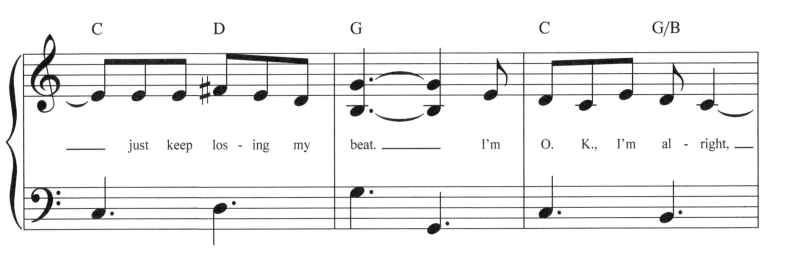

_____ just keep los - ing my beat. _____ I'm O. K., I'm al - right, _____

find me some - bod - y to love, _____ find me some -

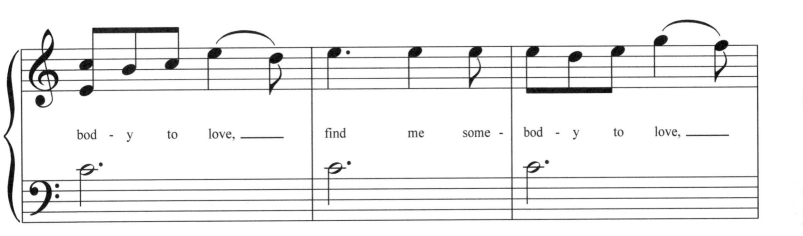

bod - y to love, _____ find me some - bod - y to love, _____

love, _____ love. _____ Find me some - bod - y to love, _____ find me some -

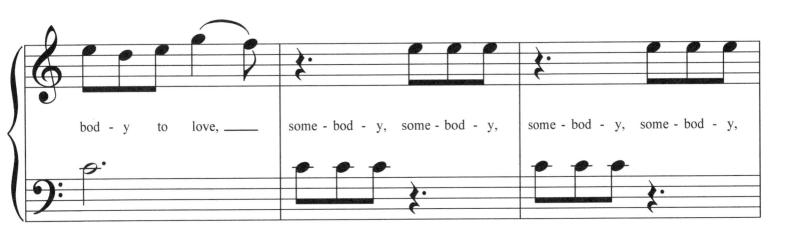

bod - y to love, _____ some - bod - y, some - bod - y, some - bod - y, some - bod - y,

some - bod - y. Find me some - bod - y, find me some - bod - y to love. Can

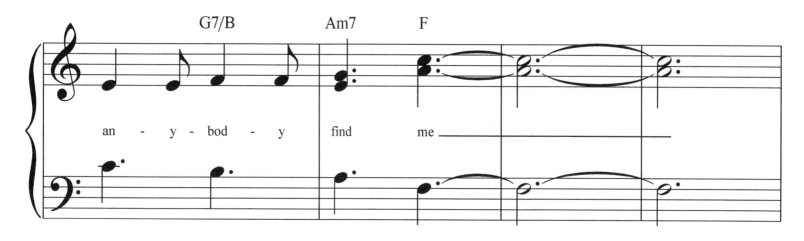

G7/B   Am7   F

an - y - bod - y find me _____

Gsus   C   C/B

some - bod - y to _____ love?

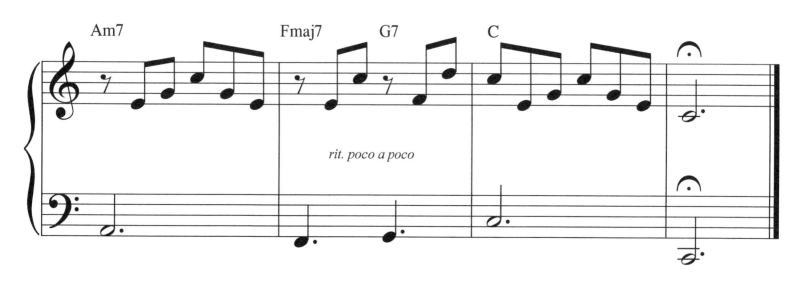

Am7   Fmaj7   G7   C

rit. poco a poco

UNDER PRESSURE

Words and Music by FREDDIE MERCURY,
JOHN DEACON, BRIAN MAY,
ROGER TAYLOR and DAVID BOWIE

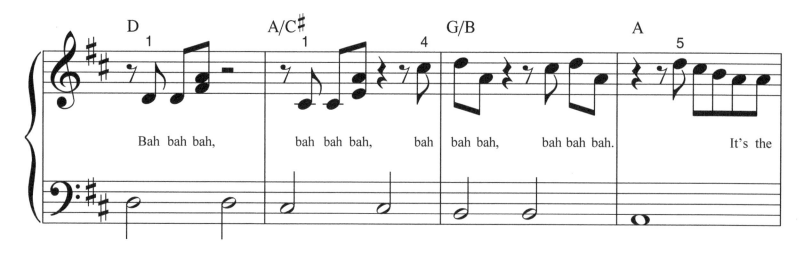

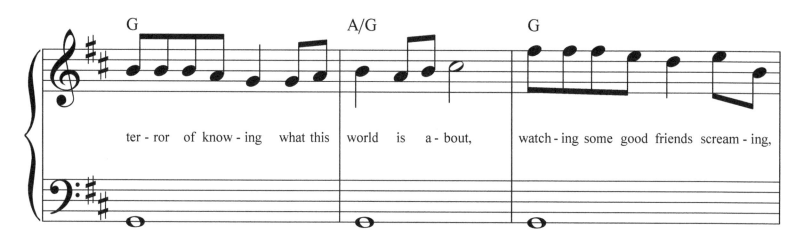

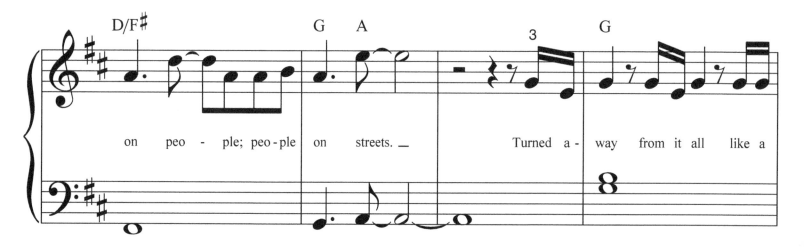

blind man; sat on a fence, but it don't work. Keep

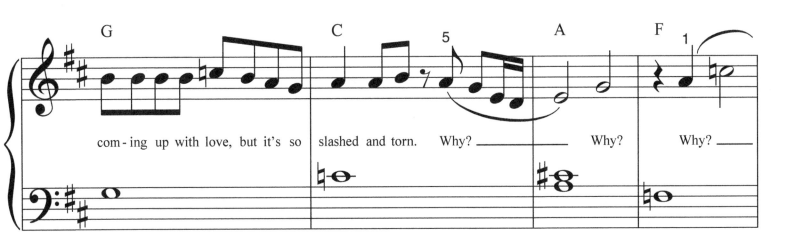

com-ing up with love, but it's so slashed and torn. Why? _____ Why? Why? _____

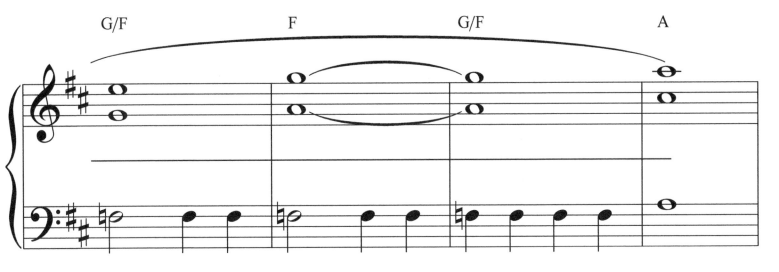

In - san - i - ty laughs, _ un - der pres - sure we're crack - ing. Can't we

give our - selves _____ one more chance? _____ Why can't we
give love _____ that one more chance? _____ Why can't we give love, give love,

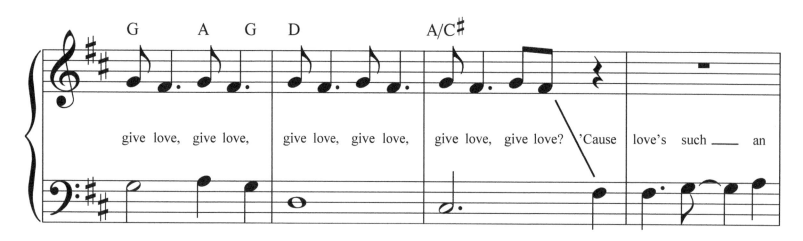

give love, give love, give love, give love, give love, give love? 'Cause love's such _____ an

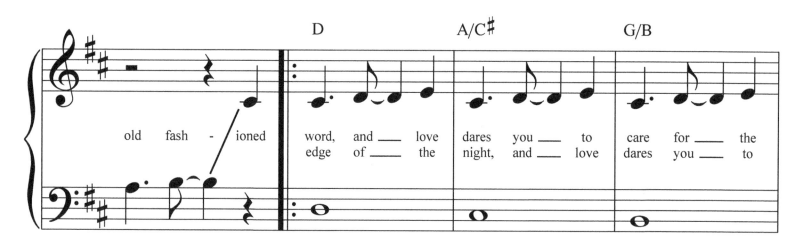

old fash - ioned word, and _____ love dares you _____ to care for _____ the
edge of _____ the night, and _____ love dares you _____ to

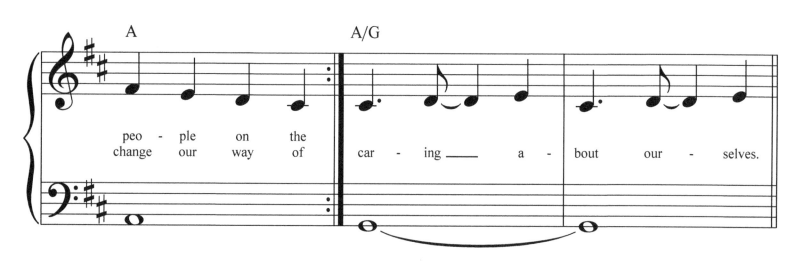

peo - ple on the
change our way of car - ing _____ a - bout our - selves.

WE ARE THE CHAMPIONS

Words and Music by
FREDDIE MERCURY

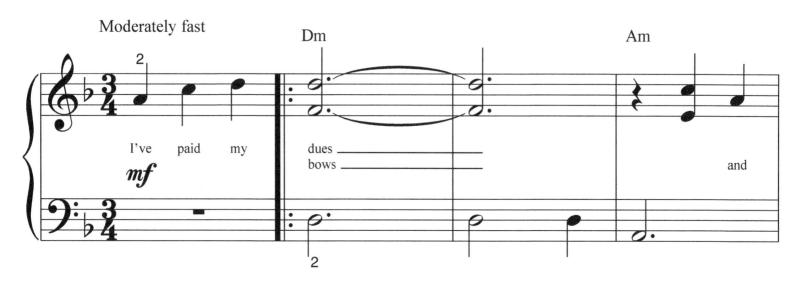

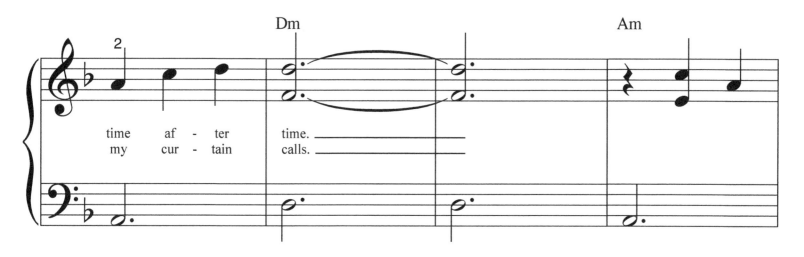

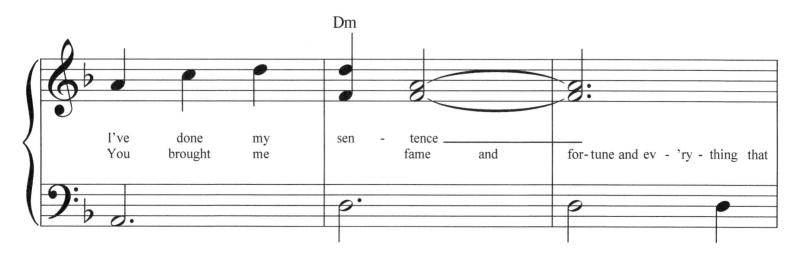

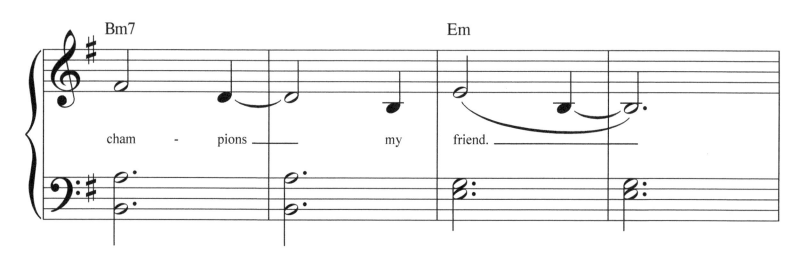

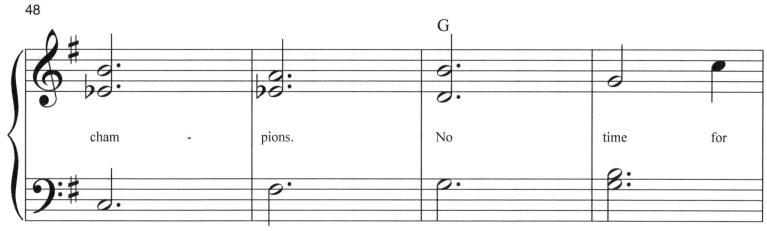

cham - pions. No time for

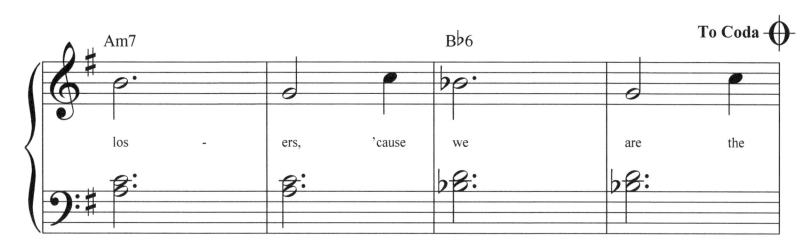

los - ers, 'cause we are the

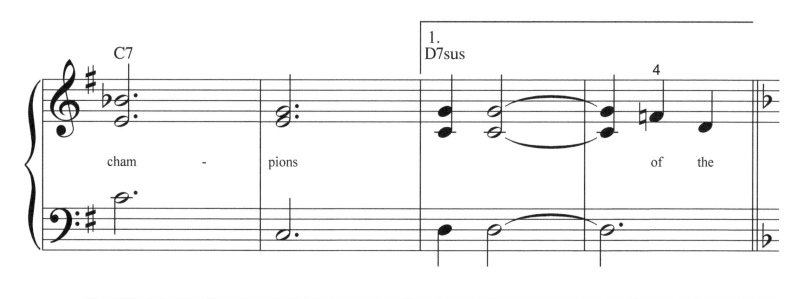

cham - pions of the

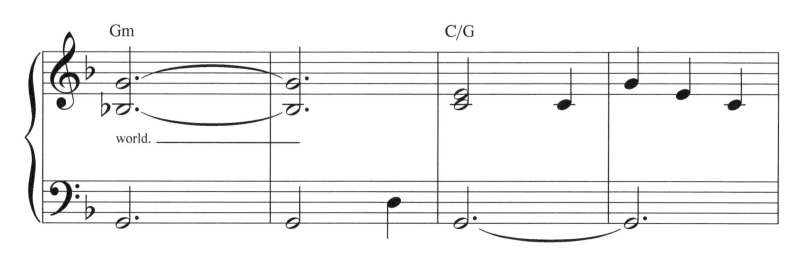

world. _____

YOU'RE MY BEST FRIEND

Words and Music by
JOHN DEACON

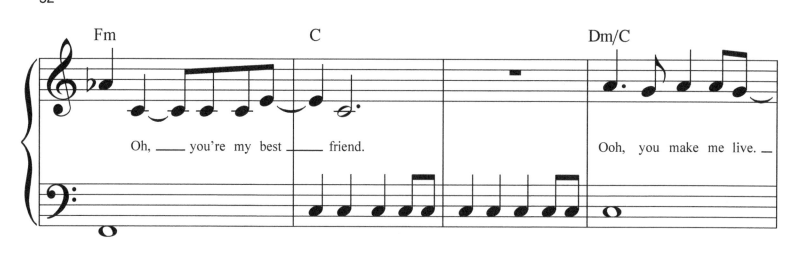

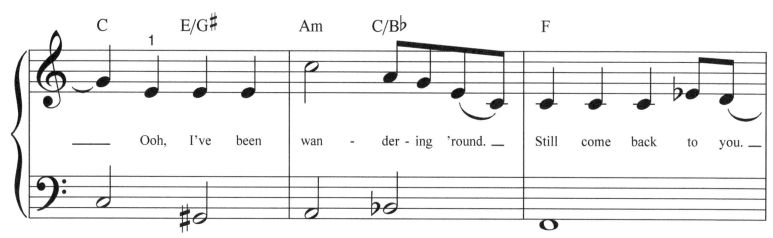

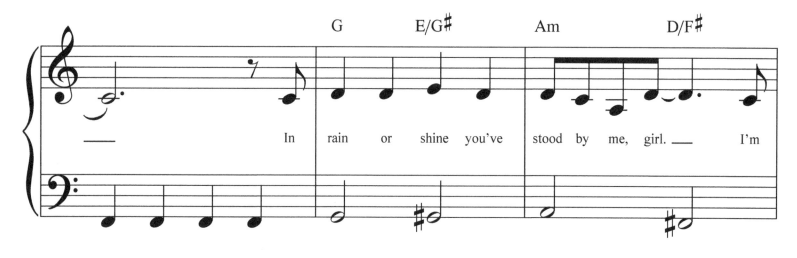

WE WILL ROCK YOU

Words and Music by
BRIAN MAY